BE HUMANE

BREAD, ARTILLERY AND LIFE.

MRINAL KANTI GUIN

Contents

Contents

Preface

My childhood dream was to create a better society. When I grew up, I saw and felt that things were not so straightforward, because at first not everyone would understand everything. If I had understood then this problem would not exist. Secondly, when I got a little older, I realized about our language. I understood the contribution of famous persons including Ishwar Chandra and Rammohun. Because not everyone can say that everything can be done. You have to write in an understandable language. So many thanks to all the great human beings. They have paved the way long ago. Thirdly, the difficulty in writing science in mother tongue is the transformation of language which is not the language but the language of the writer, because the vocabulary of english language is infinite. The scholars and writers of the world are constantly enriching this store. Fourthly, it is our responsibility to take this world society forward in tandem with the rest of the world. If we want to make the society science-minded, we have to write more and more in many language.

My first public awareness book was "Be Humane." Being published. This is my attempt to create science and awareness in the minds of the people. My aim is to widen the minds of the people so that we can live better, so that we can open the windows of the mind more, so that the light of knowledge may come.

These fifty essays are taken from different parts of life. People from all walks of life have been honoured here.

I am personally indebted to all those who have directly and indirectly helped me in writing this book. I will keep them in my heart forever.

My family and wife-daughter have always helped me mentally. This book could not have been published without their direct cooperation.

And without saying a word, everything remains incomplete. He is the publisher. I am grateful for his contribution in publishing this book.

I have full confidence in the readers in this regard. We will improve ourselves. I hope you will be by my side.

Mrinal Kanti Guin

15/03/2022

CHAPTER ONE

First light: Birds

Iam sitting on the meadow looking towards the yard. Pin drops, all around. 5:30 in the morning. The busyness of the people did not start then. Crows, sparrows, doyles, finches and storks come and sit on the neem tree in the yard. Their day has started long ago. Kingfishers are sitting quietly on the top of the bamboo tree by the side of the pond, looking towards the water of the pond. The cuckoo is calling from the baby tree a couple of times. Swan-goose water play in the pond ___. On the right side of the veranda, a leaf of a small fig tree seems to have turned upside down, unlike the other leaves. I saw very well that on that page a Moutussi is coming and going from time to time, coming and going again. At first I did not understand the reason. I realized a little better, and My goodness! So much for Mautussi's bamboo. Nice to meet you. Not to mention two more birds, the Dahuk bird, which is called white-breasted waterhen. I heard this bird is very timid. Tried many times to catch. I ran behind him many times in my childhood. Listening to my mother's words, I get traps but fail again and again. Now think of that failure but there is joy. Another bird is the jungle bubler birds , which is called seven sister bird or. Seven to eight birds live together. They have created incomparable beauty by dancing in the yard.

We all know that the birds are the unique creature that posses wings(except Ostrich). If we think about from the point of evolution, that wings are converted from front legs. Their body is warm and the bones are fluffy and filled with air. They have beaks and particularly no teeth. They can fly in the air. Some birds (like Dodo, Raphus cucullatus) that lived in the Mauritius near Madagascar become extinct. Their nature is that they could not fly properly. Particularly, Mauritius near Madagascar was densely covered with forest and other animals. Curious mind searches different places in the world. For example, Emu in Antarctica. It is particularly true in all cases. The normal features of ecology are an existence of versatile plant and animal. They are always depending on one other. There should be a perfect balance and peaceful co-existence. The main point is that they are all auto generating and the external forces are devoid of any types of pressure of that ecology. Sometimes that external force plays a vital role to control such ecology. Sometimes they become very much detrimental to the particular plants or animal. In those cases, the people may play an important role in the society. They can protect some endangered plants and animals and thereby control and restore the biodiversity in true sense. Many national and international organizations have played vital role in these aspects globally in a very effective way. For betterment of the ecology at a large, there effectively should be increased many fold. Many private and public donation or encouragement may be initiated for ourselves to maintain the biodiversity at single point of time.

CHAPTER TWO

The farmer: The in the eyes

Clouds of white clouds in the blue sky of the rain. The hopes and dreams of the farmers are filled in the running 6 cloud boats. From sowing seeds in the land to cultivation. They have a dream to bring Kharif crop at home. Jacobin cuckoo in the urge to fulfill their hopes more!
Going to the clouds, they begged for water for their favorite farmers. The wonder of human beings is that those hawk birds fly in the lap of clouds thinking maybe this-
The Kites, Birds of prey, are flying in the above which perfectly, like a symbol of seriousness in the chest of the sky.

What better way could there be than to remain steadfast in the pursuit of the goal, despite being addicted to prey? The vulture matches the cow. Wandering silently from the sky. But this bird tells a lot about the future. The cock and hen cry in the dawn are like a natural alarm. As if to say don't sleep anymore. The right time is near to awake. Awaken the thoughts of nature, as if , they want to say that we are not finished. I'm here. I am still alive, waiting for the right time to start. Will that yellow bird of guava tree come in everyone's life again? I hope so.

CHAPTER THREE

Mesmerizing memory: Birthday of Vidyasagar

Then we will barely cross the boundary of the village primary school. I hope to study in high school. Not like the other children in the village. Their common job was to help their parents in their agricultural work from childhood. As a result, they would be handcuffed in all these activities from their childhood. But now that situation has improved considerably. Boys and girls could get married and start a family at a very young age. The burden of the world would come at a very young age. Today we are feeling how many great men including Vidyasagar-Rammohun have done valuable work in this society. You can understand him many years ago because they were great men.

However, after finishing my primary school lessons in time, I was admitted to a high school near the village. Hundreds of students. It seems to be a suppressed fear. I can.

You have to walk two or three miles. Raw road. Knee-deep mud in the rain. No vehicles. Only buffalo or bullock carts go. One of the attractions of that earthy soil rain was to many.

People were much simpler. The days would go by to provide for one's own food. It seemed that there was not so much disease and plague as there is today. Basil, and other medicinal plants were grown in the meadows are also appreciated.

It is true that we have moved forward. Lost and some priceless gems.

CHAPTER FOUR

Suddenly (An Awareness Article)

Let us know something new today. We didn't eat much on the street. Many times to satisfy hunger, many times to greed, many times to intoxication, many times after deliberate excitement.

The first meal is logical. The hunger of the body has to be satisfied otherwise many bad things can happen. Others can often cause harm in life or even death.

Lots of things are sold on the street, which makes the tongue water. Even if I don't need to, I go to eat later in greed without knowing anything.

For example, consuming a Star fruit (Averrhoa carambola is a scientific name.) I don't know what happens to you.

The fruit is quite tasty to eat. There are a few very good qualities. That is not what we are talking about today. In some cases, people may die playing this fruit.

This Star fruit contains a substance called oxalic acid and

caramboxin. This caramboxin causes severe damage to the nervous system and kidneys.

This oxalic acid accumulates in the kidneys in the form of oxalate. So those who have kidney problems - think a little before eating the fruit. Everyone will be fine. Be aware.

CHAPTER FIVE

Bat and Corona: A discussion

The Corona epidemic has changed a lot in our lives. Many can't stand that ____.

Many people say or believe that corona is the product of this disease. There has been a lot of debate about this or it is still going on. Everything will be known in the future. We haven't reached that place yet.

We are talking about Bat. This means great bat and small bat in a big sense. In taxonomy they are included in the order Chiroptera. Whose meaning is transformed into hand fan or wing. Bat is the only mammal. The word Chiro comes from the Greek, meaning hand. The word ptera means wing. They are divided into megakiroptera and microchiroptera. They all love nocturnal and dark. Bat survives by eating fruits such as palms, guavas, etc. It also eats some spiders, insects. They help in pollination of some plants and transport of seeds. The production and growth of many equatorial plants depend solely on bats. They all live in nocturnal and dark caves. Guano fertilizer is produced from their excrement or feces. They are carriers of many diseases, such as rabies. Now many claim corona disease. Which is burning the whole world now? We are helplessly forced to bow to it. But hopefully we can bring Corona under complete control.

We have seen them in our house in the holes and where there is less light during the day. I closed all the hustle and bustle of the house and said goodbye to them with respect. The Western Countries consider the Bat as a source of evil energy. (Bats are potentially associated with darkness, malevolence, witchcraft, vampires and ultimately death.) Many believe Bat can't see, that's not true at all. Bat's life is black and white. Bat only see black and white. The most surprising thing is that people can feel a lot of light waves that they can't feel, which means that light-colored light waves are not the visible boundary of their eyes at all. The border is much bigger. The blood-eating vampire is but a kind of vulture.
So it is wise to stay away from all these animals. Isn't that so?

We know that bats are the winged animal that can fly because their fore limbs (called patagium Plural- patagia) converted into small winged like structure. These limbs not only helped during the flight but also often act like sensory organ that can sense the presence of different object from the distance. These apparently seems strange but play very important role of their nocturnal habit. The winged fore-limbs although have some uncommon features that are unlike the forelimbs of the birds but plays important role in flight as well as other important physical works like sense the atmospheric temperature and presence of any dangerous matter.

Many think that these bats often plays very important role as discussed earlier but the production of many crops varies with the pollination. As sometimes bats are considered as potential pollinators of certain crops like many night flowering plants (Mangoes, Bananas and Guava). The flowers that are visited by bats are typically: i) open at night; ii) Large in size (1 to 3.5 inches); iii) Pale or white in color; iv)Very fragrant, a fermenting or fruit-like odor; and/or v) Copious dilute nectar.

Bats feed on the insects in the flowers as well as on the nectar and flower parts, such as calabash, sausage tree, areca palm, kapok tree, and banana. So, considering all aspects of the Bats, we should not afraid from the bat. Rather we should be happy in seeing the hanging bats from the trees during the day times. Based on the size as described by the scientists, they have several hundreds of species as live around the world. Some are voracious feeder of nectars and some otherwise feed on insects. Normally they do not attack the humans and always wanted to remain aloof from the human beings. As a result of these, we found them in the crevices. They are typically a mammal that can fly due to their patagia. So, normally a bat, when fly can make a high pitch sound as they make these high-pitched sounds, too high for us to hear, but when their cries ricochet off distant objects, the echoes tell them there's a house over there, a tree in front of them, a moth flying over on the left and so on and so they "see" by echolocation.

Further reading

Bats (Chiroptera) as vectors of diseases and parasites

Facts and Myths

Editors

Sven Klimpel

Heinz Mehlhorn

CHAPTER SIX

Safe Water : Good health

We all know that water is very much indispensable for our body. It is true for in both case of animal and plants kingdom. From micro-organism to multi cellular organisms, this apparently liquid molecule plays significant role in their life. Water is often considered synonymous with life. In inorganic chemistry, the simple systematic name for water, H2O is called hydrogen Oxide. We all know that no plant or animal can survive on this earth without water. If we do not save this water day by day, then we have to be thrilled to think that the terrible day is coming. It should be borne into mind that not all water of the earth is consumable. The water present in the ocean and sea are salty and not fit for drink. In normal occurrence, the the water are dirty and filled with various microbes such as bacteria, fungi and other poisonous substances. So, utmost care should be taken for selection of water fit for consumption. It is pity for the normal citizen, even for the developed countries, we have failed miserably to supply the safe potable drinking water. We, although, know that water harbours different causal meant for different diseases. Some of them are as harmful as they can put the human life in danger and hence need serious concern for that matter.

Some organizations have already started raising awareness about water. This work is also being done by the government but the people need to be more aware and vigilant for themselves.

The water we drink or the water we should cook in is called pure drinking water or potable water. What the World Health Organization (WHO) says as the standard of water is not recognized in all countries.

So it is very difficult to say which is the standard or its equivalent. Different organizations laid down different standards which sometimes confusing to accept for the common people.

Several developed countries, including Australia, the European Union, and the United States, have set the standard for drinking water for their people.
Here are some things to keep in mind:
1) Drinking water should be germ free.
2) According to Bureau of Indian Standard (BIS) of India, Total Dissolved Solids (TDS) limit is 500 ppm, but according to WHO, TDS limit is 300 ppm.
3) Must be free of Arsenic and Silica.
4) The pH should be between 6.5 to 8.5.
Many of us know that there are many water borne diseases like cholera, typhoid, diarrhea, dysentery, polio, meningitis. Also, bathing in dirty water can lead to trachoma, a contagious disease of the eye. In other words, it is easy to understand that drinking clean water will not cause all these diseases. So everyone should drink pure water as

much as possible.

Many people believe that they will drink pure water but they will wash the utensils in dirty water. Therefore, different analysts think that this issue is also equally important to maintain proper human hygiene. Raising awareness of the issue can only be effective measures. So we have to think about water conservation. Adequate rainfall water should be kept in ponds or reservoirs or artificially used for cultivation and at the same time dependence on ground water for cultivation should be reduced. With proper planning, there is a possibility of this. We have to save our water resources. We hope that our small efforts will be the beginning of a great work. Everyone must come forward at all levels by raising public awareness. We will take responsibility to protect our future generations.

It will be reflected in the future when well-meaning people understand it.

These main categories are a useful place to start for building good hygiene habits:

i) Shower hygiene, ii) Nail hygiene, iii) Teeth hygiene, iv) Toilet hygiene-Wash your hands after you use the restroom, v) Hands hygiene and vi) Sickness hygiene.

Always apply your positive thought to be safe for yourself and your surroundings.

CHAPTER SEVEN

The feet are then on the ground: Humility

From ancient times the people of the world have heard different kinds of sounds. The curious mind has gone in search of its source. They have found the genuine source that attracts our mind. Some words are natural, some are artificial.

Well, have you ever wondered how those who are blind perceive or understand the things that are scattered around them?

Their ears and noses do a lot of that. Let's talk about those words. When we have previous experience with sound, our brain looks at it and has a real idea about sound.

What if you don't have previous experience?

Then we say, the word is like a word we know. We do not have the experience at this time so we can understand and analyze it differently. Isn't it? Well what is that word actually, for which so much is arranged?

Sound is a form of energy that is transmitted by vibrations in the form of waves through gases, liquids and solids. Through the air, sound can travel up to 344 meters per second. This is called a Mac speed. Mac units are used in the shipbuilding industry of rockets, jets, missiles (missiles).

Well, have you ever thought that this word sounds good and annoying at times? Not so.

Very true. Because sweet words make the human brain feels good. Such as music. And everyone knows the reason for being annoyed by harsh words.

Well these are all but we hear.

There may be things that are beyond our hearing. We don't hear them, but dogs, cats, bats and other animals do.

Just think?

We are not the best creatures in the world, actually. Which is because the human brain has the ability to analyze events in depth? The ability to understand which is good and which is bad and Ability to plan perfectly. It is very important to awaken the conscience of the heart once again.

The best of man, not above him.

Curiosity matters most.

CHAPTER EIGHT

My country: My priority

Well, we all know that India has been ruled by the British for more than 200 years. It is taught in history. We read. The struggle for independence and its history is also taught in the history of our country so that we have a thorough knowledge.
One thing you have noticed while reading is that most of the freedom fighters are Bengalis. Whose name do I exclude?!

It had to gain the most momentum but the British, because they wanted to rule India. They have all seen and become apprehensive of the knowledge, intellect, discipline, unity, spiritual fortitude, indomitable perseverance of the Bengali nation. As a result, we saw the Partition of Bengal in 1905 and we have suffered its history and its evils. The British realized long ago that keeping intelligent Bengalis together would not be of any benefit to the British at all. Because they came to establish business in this country. Not for development or service. To exploit and to develop their own country Britain.

Those revolutionaries stood in the way of their plan. They were proud and dedicated to the cause of patriotism.

Remember that today and all the people of the world respect Bengalis.
Today I will tell you a great story.
It is about the Germans!!

We know about their notoriety. After thinking of a person, Hitler!
After the tragic defeat in World War II, the Potsdam Conference took place. We all know that.
We know that Germany was a strong industrialized country. They are very much punctual and great amount of self respect that matters most for the uprising of a country form the very beginning. In a nut shell, the world most prominent power, at that time, become very much angry with that particular nation for their vehemenous nature. I personally oppose this very much. In spite of all these, they have some best qualities that the world should teach from them, that is their love for their mother land, only because of these quality, the notorious HITLER, abuse these ethnic class so badly. The rest of the world were very much curious about the post WW-II period. As a result of these consequences, the main purpose of the conference was to destroy all heavy industries and to encourage agro-based industries and to transform the Germans into a working class.

After World War II, the country was divided into four parts to weaken its power. Its control distributed with the former Soviet Union (Present day RUSSIA), Britain, France and the United States, respectively.
There is no need to give details of what they did to the Germans at that time. In a word, they have done everything in a democratic way to destroy that nation in a scientific

manner.
History speaks.
However, on May 23, 1949, the Federal Republic of Germany (FRG) or West Germany was formed, which was largely influenced by France and the United States. Its capital is Bonn. The seed of a tree germinate at that point of time which started to flourish gradually as the times fly.

The German Democratic Republic, or East Germany, was formed on October 7, 1949, under the influence of the former Soviet Union. Berlin is its capital. Another hopes for the future nation become uprising.

During the Cold War, the two Germans fought and clashed with each other. So much bloodshed was there.
But that scenario has changed completely after Soviet Russia collapsed. With the passage of time, new power house become generated from the ashes and they have their spectacular uprising that whole world about to receive a new power.

West Germany became part of the European Union subsequently and East Germany was liberated from Russian influence. A great coincidence occurs subsequently.
Talks between the two German nations began in the national level.
Since the two German nations speak German, their food and culture are the same, so October 3, 1990 (Unification Day) has come together. Their ethnic class was also the same. They become united. What a great uprising! Isn't it?

The new country is called the Federal Republic of Germany, with Berlin as its capital.

Since then, Germany has become a developed country on the map of Europe and the world, because they are an enterprising, hardworking nation and they cooperate with each other and strictly follow the rules for the development of the country and society.

I think this is instructive for them. Isn't that so?

We know history repeats itself.

Now the Germen are considered with deep respect throughout the world. Even their enemies forced to respect them because of their character, boldness, truthfulness and above all punctuality. They not only developed themselves but in the same time have set a perfect example for the others to love the country first. My country: My priority.

CHAPTER NINE

Wherever the eye goes: Friends

The main function of all languages is to express the thoughts in the right way. In some cases, human emotions have to be expressed in words, deeds and different types of body gestures also are used carefully that deemed fit for the particular purpose. In these cases, talking is a kind of expression that we want to relate with the audience. The personality of a person, the manner of speaking, the speed of speaking, the humour mixed in doing, the level of tone of voice while speaking also depend a lot. The charismatic deliver of such things matters most. The gestures of the mind can be expressed in the right way with the gestures of the eyes, the hands and the feet and the body without speaking. Yeah all that sounds pretty crap to me, Looks like for me either. Not so:: Why? Can you tell me in details?

But we don't have to teach it. Since English is our mother tongue, it is very much our birth. There is no need to go into the details of what is known as non-verbal communication in English.

This type of communication is one of the most important

languages in almost all languages of the world. It is surprising to think that the same thing gives different ideas to different people.

Many times people do this kind of non verbal communication even on the ability of the person who is with him to understand because there is another perception of happiness in it. It also releases the pleasure hormone oxytocin in the human body. This, of course, made the video an overnight sensation.

However, in the case of a liar, none of this works. So liars should be careful for themselves. You may be cheating on the person in front of you, you may remember, but at the same time you are slowly damaging the vital organs of your body, causing many serious diseases including high blood pressure to take up residence in your body. In a special relationship like conjugal relationship between husband and wife or girl friend, this types of special expression matters most for long lasting relationship. Some become more compatible with the passage of time. During sex, these types of non verbal communication, many times, increase the pleasure or enjoyment. Often, the partners unknowingly responded it with full of emotion. So in it, these types of emotion often mixed with the primitive types of language long before the discovery of alphabet and language. We should keep in mind that. Some mime act often represents the same. An eminent mime actors like Charlie Chaplin can express almost all types of talking without speaking a single word. Charlie Chaplin, the famous actor has proved that expression without making a sound may be a great medium for proper understanding and there would be no language barrier. Be it French,

English or Russian, every citizen can understand the inner meaning quietly without any hustle.

So before telling a lie, think for yourself. You just have to be more discriminating with the help you render toward other people. You may not understand today. If the matter goes on for a long time, does anyone know what the result will be? These continuous actions of telling false matter to another person may harm you both mentally and physically. If you think about your mental condition which is very important matter for your mental peace of mind and which also connects to your bodily environment which may directly link up with the longevity of a person. So, if you want to stay longer in this beautiful earth happily, abstain from the false world, fake people or anything bad for your personal and mental health. Be happy and remain happy for ever and live peacefully and be disease free.
At no time does nature change its rules.

CHAPTER TEN

It was twelve o'clock: Little tricky

How much work do we have? Many times it is difficult to imagine. Then if you keep your head cool and stop thinking and do the work one by one, you will see that the work has been done for a while. The first thing you need to do is plan. The more perfect the plan, the more successful the person will be in his personal life. Unplanned mentality is the name of stagnation.

The most important thing when planning is to keep a cool head.
If a person can do this work while planning and implementing it, then 90% of it becomes his work.
In addition, each member of the team needs to have a complete knowledge or idea about the type of work and the objective.

Everyone has to give 100% time to that work so that the work can be completed on time or before the time.
Whether or not a task will be successful depends on the body language of the team leader because if the team leader believes that a task will be done in the right way at the

right time, then no one can stop the task, because the team leader's confidence becomes the confidence of every member. And who can stop him when he has confidence in any work?

Your actions today will help you build your future. My actions are mine.
There is no easy way to success; there is no shortcut in success.
No great work can be done by cunning. I believe in my own life.
But in every case we have to keep in mind that there are some cunning people everywhere.
For all those people, 'the clock is twelve'.

Do not understand!
That is, when you realize that the gentleman in front of you is jealous of your progress, then you have to find a way to survive in this world.
'It was twelve o'clock,' he said.
Funny thing is not so.
I think "Strong dedication with integrity to work is the key of every success"
What do you say?
Obstacles will come, hey! That's the real fun of winning. The more obstacles in that work, the greater the joy of being successful in that work.
Duty with determination, dedication is the only key to winning any job.

CHAPTER ELEVEN

Seeing with the ears:How?

"Tell me what you think so much?" Jane said to Timothy Stern.
"Nothing." The answer came.
Timothy Stern thinks but the thought is still there.
The relationship between the two is but father and daughter. Very good.
Jane was very good at studying. She is currently a successful person. Earns well. Dad made people with improved reforms. A great physician.

But when she was young, her mother was just different. A self-absorbed person. Everyone believed without judgment analysis.
As a child, Jane used to enjoy playing with other small children in her village home.
Her mind would be overwhelmed with joy. She used to play many games including slingshot and thief police.
Every time after the game, his mother wanted to know the result of that game.
Never said "Mom I lost the game."

Sometimes she would say, "Mom, I would have won if I had a little more time" or sometimes she would say "I would have won if I practice well for little more."
From an early age, Jane seemed to carry a triumphant insistence in her mind. It was very energetic to see as a father.

So when she didn't want to eat, the father would start a competition to trick her into eating. He used to say, "Jane is the last to eat food and she will finish eating at last!"
Where does the business go!

In the absence of all, father and daughter have sown the seeds of a strange competition. In which Jane unknowingly increased the efficiency of her brain and it is still doing so.
Mother passed away last time in Corona but she did not give up.

Everyone then served the patients like heroines, fearing for their lives. Her father's words still ring in her ears. That mother's love increases the power of the brain and soaks the mind.
Now her father is bed ridden. Can't talk even;
Even so, owning one is still beyond the reach of the average person.
So all these people are completely influenced by their surroundings.

CHAPTER TWELVE

Medal: The chain of success

"Uncle, look at this!" Brian grabbed Dillon. Memorial and certificate of his Math Olympiad in hand, of inter-national level.

Dillon is the second of three brothers in the house. Age forty-seven. Brian is the only son of the family. Age thirteen.

He has been a very affectionate person since childhood. Brilliant in study! Great affection of the neighborhood and the locals. Many people from the area have come to Brian's house today to encourage him. Everyone is encouraging; someone wants to know about his future plans again.

Some people in the area are also comparing Brian with some of their close relatives.

His parents were happy with his son's success.

The house is almost festive.

Suddenly there were tears in Dillon's eyes.

Unable to stay, Elder brother said, "What happened Dillon! I remember again!"

Tears welled up in the eyes of both of them as they said "yes".

Everyone who came home was shocked. What's the matter!

On this happy day ----!
One of them said, "I remember Bob! He is the youngest son of this family. He is very talented.
Everyone in the area was very happy. We even ate sweets when it happened.
Everyone is happy with his success. Surely, when he grows up, he will brighten the face of the area.
The bike was barely bought at home. The two brothers were overjoyed!
The two brothers are growing.
They decided to bring the national Scholarship Certificate and Scholarship from District Inspector of School office. By bike.
But alas! On the way! He collided head-on with a moving bus at a bend in the road. He never returned. He left for the land of no return. Those memories remained later.
Sometimes he gets scared. I think of that brother.
So what are these tears of joy! Not anything else.
At home, therefore, there was a lack of joy.
I don’t know what happened after that.
Only the mind was burdened.
What is invisible in my eyes?
I just told Brian "May God bless you!"

CHAPTER THIRTEEN

Must be: An event

Melia, the only daughter of the joint family. Age is now ten. Her father has four brothers. Everyone has a child. A boy. Understandably, she is getting a little more affection than others. A little emotional, eager to speak out against injustice. Grandma's eyeballs. Grandpa's darling little sister. The difficult reality of society is elusive to her.

Aunt Victoria did not always look well. Because she wanted the girl to be acquainted with reality, not with illusion. Be familiar with education, not with superstition. Be familiar with new science, not with advertising and falsehood. So she could not help but look at her mother-in-law's granddaughter and said, "Mother, tells the child to read once."

And where does it go!

Kurukshetra, all types of vandalism started!

Someone said, "eight or ten years and so on-- . You will marry your granddaughter; see a well-earned and established groom. The solution to all problems will end at once."

Melia did not understand about the unknown partner.

She just shouted, "No, never. I shall kill you all"

By then Grandma's become pacified.

She said- "That's right! Why would that be? She becomes

self-reliant first. Then something else."

"Then tell your granddaughter to read a little along with rapt attention. She doesn't listen to us, only listen to you, ma. If you want her well."

Three generations of discussions or quarrels at home, whatever you say, it was fun and enjoyable for some people in the neighbourhood.

Many enjoyed the affair. Some would say - "Drama."

Then eight more years passed.

Now she analyzes her own good and bad judgment.

Persevering.

Grandpa said one day- "Then I, I, T (Indian Institute of Technology) is there!"

The proud granddaughter said- "Yes!"

Twelve more years have passed.

One day, out of curiosity, Victoria went to Melia and said, "What happened! You have changed so much. She is so persistent. So attentive. She is so successful."

She just said - "The day Grandma told the story, I told your father to have a determination of sex test before you were born, but your father didn't listen. That day I made a promise in my heart. I will show success, I shall show to the world that nothing in the world will dependent on gender."

And asked Victoria- "You all have one son. Did you go for test or not?"

Aunt did not answer.

She just angrily answered that is why she is so angry with that whoreson.

CHAPTER FOURTEEN

Value yourself: Your pride

"Sit in that chair. Don't run around too much." George said to Harry. So I sat down and thought to myself, yes! Tuition will still be earned again. The last five days did not go to teach. Tomorrow is the last day of the month. The incident happened about fifteen days in this month. Who knows what the fathers of the students will think? Will I get paid in a month?

And he said in his mouth- "Grandpa is coming! An urgent work has been done. Can't it be done in a hurry? Do you think I can pay that five thousand dollar now?"

"What's the matter with the money and the tree? I kept telling someone. I don't see that chap. Tell me what to do?" George said in his mouth and thought to himself that if he lends to those needy people, he will not be able to pay it back.

What does it look like not to say on the face. Then I call him happily and sadly.

By now Harry has known his mind. "No, brother! No, I'm going, it is too late for Me." he said and left. There is no way to recognize people if they are not in danger. I have done much for him during his rainy days. Nowadays, what I

expect in return is wrong.
He could not accept the incident in any way.
I have to lie to my mother again. Mom was supposed to visit the doctor tomorrow. I have changed the day to the doctor three times with this. Mother is suffering from leg pain. Not seen anymore, so much suffering; but mother always remains Culm and suffers happily. I am in this situation for just how much money. I am ashamed to think so.
Tears well up in his eyes as he thinks of all these.
Anyway, you have to earn more. Otherwise life has no value. On an empty stomach and empty pockets, the world actually looks different.
There is no place for education and knowledge.
Only after remembering my father's words.
Dad used to say- "Time is priceless. He who learns not to pay the price of time can never improve his life. He himself is hostile to the God and to him. Time can fix everything. So time should never be wasted."
Alas! If I had obeyed my father's words, my mother would have received such treatment and I would have a family today.
Now I understand - "History remembers the successful and teaches others."

CHAPTER FIFTEEN

Afternoon: An accident

"Why didn't Danish come to visit today? Let's find out what happened to him." I told Ashton.

Three bosom friends. I will give the school final this year. After studying all day, I go out in the afternoon to get some air. The three of us walk together and discuss various things. Tests, future plans and a lot of time just chat.

I spend a lot of time walking along the village road to talk about the future of the village. The news that comes out on the radio and in the newspapers is also in the discussion. No one gets a good night's sleep unless three people get together at the end of the day. This is like an attraction or infallible intoxication.

"Come on. Let's see." - The two of them went to his house in search of Danish.

I tried to find out about him from a few people but no one knew about him.

So I necessarily reached his house. Then of course there was no mobile like today. Many of us know about fifty years ago. Then the social management! The friendship was pure. The number of friends was low but the heart was similar.

I see his father is lying. People are giggling at home. Everyone is asking for his face. Suddenly village head of the neighborhood said, "What are you looking at him? Don't you see that the snake has bitten him? Call the Ojha." Danish's stepmother is staring blankly. Stunned. The stepbrother is shouting loudly and saying - "What happened to Dad! Why aren't you talking?"

Make the scene.

We are young. Do you know what to do? But thinking about my dear friend, I said, "Why the Ojha? Let's go to the hospital." That scene cannot be seen!

His father loves our friend and his elder son. It was like a spiritual relationship.

I thought, who does not know what will happen if you take like these useless fellow?

The argument must start! Thc journey started after about two hours and when I reached Prince Hospital it was 11 PM. I don't know what to do. Insane. Looking for a doctor.

The doctor came, checked the patient. When I saw him leaving without saying a word, I said, "How did you see, Doctor?"

He shouted in anger in deep anguish, "I had to bring it later! You had no sense"

Hearing this, I cannot stop my tears. It rolls down my cheeks, as if I had to cry in deep agony.

It is still a pity. My eyes still fill with water for this reason.

It is very pertinent to speak that the humanity and it should be above all consideration. We should think for ourselves first. This is normal and nothing wrong in it. People in all times normally don't think for other and it would be difficult to bear these people. We should be against malnourishment, ill talks and corruptions. Some plays important roles in society. As a result of which our society have been benefitted much. A lot of human either directly or indirectly benefitted in it. In long run, if this continues, a great future would be there. There will be less crime against child and women and low corruption rate. Every good thing in the society should be encouraged in all level of society and bad things should be severely punished or discouraged.

CHAPTER SIXTEEN

Heart made of stone?

"Hey, move away! You can't see the boy in his eyes. He will eat." - This is what Mea's mother was saying. To her daughter.

She came to her father's house during worship. She came here for a few days. Stay there will be a few more days. Her seven-month-old son in her lap. Her son crying for two days, the reason is unknown.

No one in the neighborhood tends to study. Eats day after day and sit idle and do nothing for future. Hence, they fail to generate income for them. if anybody advice them to study, they become angry because it is beyond their general custom.

"Keep saying these things. if you can arrange for food for us, we all listen to you, you don't understand that. This study is for only you. "It is because that they failed to earn their basic need easily. It is really a miserable event for the mankind.

Their words pierced her chest like a sharpened weapon. Silent and speechless.

I kept blaming myself in my mind, but I said in my mouth- "Why are you hiding the baby from John's mother like that? I heard her mother loves the baby!"

Hearing those words of mine, she got angry and shouted

and said- "Love is not ashes! Yesterday she mike's milch cow become sick. His cow used to generate three kilos of milk. What happens? Gunin (Witchcraft) came yesterday and said that there are as many problems for her in the neighborhood. "

I was shocked to hear her. I said - "Is that so? Terrible thing. What will happen then?"

I heard that Mike and his family went to John's house and had a heated argument but I don't know the details. I was a little surprised to know all that.

Joy is my peer. I did not know such orthodoxy.

John's mother has become nightmare! The weak and calm fellow has become very weak due to the smoke of fasting and fasting!

In this opportunity, the cunning fellow has been able to earn some money.

About ten more days have passed.

Now is the time to change the seasons, everyone has some or the other problem. So tell me how reasonable it is to blame someone else for this change.

And I think if the problem of the cow. They should visit to a veterinarian, the problem will be solved easily, but he does not-

Yes Ray. Still going.

John's mother is fighting to the death at Don Bosco Hospital.

It is still going on in the same way like the past. It seems that the world is not move towards the future here.

"I wonder how reasonable it is for us to brag and bow our heads in shame!"

CHAPTER SEVENTEEN

Let bow down: Upliftment

After shaking for a while, Tim said, "Sir, I will open the door of the office a little."

Being Tim, Arambagh Orderly to the Block development Officer. Expert in almost all subjects. Doesn't he know?

Sometimes I was shocked to see his real experience. I thought, how! What infinite courage. What a word. When a person came to the office, thousands of questions would plague him!

When everything was known, he would come and say to me, "Sir, many people have come, everyone, with the information they need.

One or two came, for some reasons; I took their application for further process. "

The work of the office inquiry counter would have been a lot like this.

Sometimes he would come and try to appease me and say, "Sir, tell me! I'm your man. I don't care what anyone says outside."

When I used to say these things, I understood that there must be some need, but then I just heard him not saying anything, after saying this for a while, the real purpose would come out.

Maybe he would say- "Sir! I'll be out a little earlier today, or I'll be a little late tomorrow or I want some leave from the office, etc__"

I would have understood his every word just before.

Such a strange and skilled man comes and says - "Someone has come, she wants to meet you!"

I thought maybe the house is damaged, you want a house or you want a tarpaulin or something else, because there was a flood a few days ago, it's not strange for someone like that to come! "

I had a job in hand and I told her to call her.

Orderly opened the door. The woman entered the office but did not enter the office chamber. She stared at me for a minute and left.

I have never encountered such an incident in my many years of service life.

I wanted to know what the matter is.

Head clerk of the office said, she is one of his grandsons Want to become a civil service officer. The grandson is too young! It will be four or five years.

She did not tell her grandson the story of some nonsense matter. Said the story of the country and the successful person who laid their hands for the betterment of the country.

Said the story of people engaged in the development of society.

I said, "As far as I know, people now want to make their children doctors and engineers, and they all say that when they grow up, they will serve the rural poor for free and improve the country."

He smiled and said - "Service! See Mike's advertisement. He'll come and see the patient one day a month."

I said - "Free!"

This time Tim said in his manner- "Then what would be the advertisement for Mike?"

I am proud to see such humble behaviour of people. There is some notable civil servent in the world that make us proud. They lend their brain to uplift the standard of the common people. A great deal was there for such incident through the life or the common people. I must salute them for their humble behaviour and what not?

Now, I enjoy myself thinking of myself as a civil serviceman.

That incident in the office made me more humble. This made me more responsible.

CHAPTER EIGHTEEN

Standard

Monty should not be run so slowly. A little more.
"Okay Sir," he said.
He increased the speed of the car. Speed increased from forty to seventy per hour.
I said- be careful.
There is an urgent need for my urgent official work to reach to a place.
Sudden flooding has occurred in the area but a temporary bamboo bridge in the river and a large mound of mud on both sides of it has grown. Due to this, the water is not flowing properly through the river.
Other debris, including water hyacinth, has accumulated along the middle of the river because the river does not carry water all year round.
The river has lost its normal flow. So people living on both banks of the river have forgotten the existence of the river.
"Nature doesn't listen to anyone, we have to obey nature, and they have forgotten that."
There is a temporary bamboo bridge for crossing the river.
In the rainy season, that bridge is the cause of everyone's sorrow. At other times, the bridge is the only means of transportation on both sides. It costs twenty rupees for each movement.

Everyone knows the partisan reason to keep that part of the money that goes to the temporary bridge even during the flood.

In order to keep it with all the strength of a group of people, if someone dies in the flood or someone's crop is destroyed or someone's house is submerged or someone's cattle dies, they do not leave any mark on their mind.

When I arrived, I saw a heated argument between the two sides. No one wants to listen to the heart. Both sides are adamant in their decision.

Meanwhile, the river water is rising in the rainy season.

Excitement.

One group is in crisis of its own existence.

The other side is busy packing their own sugarcane.

Even ignorant people know what to do in such a situation.

The problem starts when the personal interests of the particular person are involved in making the decision.

This is exactly the beginning of the story.

Then the judgment is not analyzed. It's a comedy, it's a weird competition.

At that time every person is no longer human anyway

Crisis of religion.

The bridge builders are strong here and the flood affected areas are weak.

Doing the right thing by analyzing justice can lead to personal danger.

Here we have to stand by the flood affected people with the identity of prudence.

So it is necessary to climb on top of the boat and try to cut with automatic saw machine and in many cases success.

I knew the power of the speed of the water - if the weak bridge is cut a little will survive?

Such wisdom can be understood from experience.

When I was about to cut it, the bridge builder was making other attempts.

I knew God was with me when people were trying to do the right thing.

The effort must be honest, so no task seems impossible. You have to stick to the work from beginning to end. Nature will always be with the honest seeker, never leave.

Phones of flood victims. Their assurance.

I knew it would take two hours.

It was one o'clock at night.

Sir, it's done. That's where we sawed.

I thought and once again it was proved that God lives in courage and truth.

This journey freed a huge area from floods.

CHAPTER NINETEEN

Life is dawn

Then I was sitting with my friends. In Kolkata, Everyone is planning their own future. The study is almost over. There is infinite uncertainty ahead of our future. We all are very much thoughtful after completion of our study. Many friends already started to earn. Some of them are now already married and have some family burden of their shoulder. They are very much come to the reality of the world. They already acquainted with the present situation of the world. They know that nobody will come to save you in rainy days. So you have to store some penny for the future. People will encourage you to get success but very small percentage of the will come forward to help you when you need them badly. It is true fact indeed.

It is hard to think that the study that I gave my mind to invent something new, I have to put an end to it. One hundred percent.

Never thought of anything else. When I saw school teachers as a child, I was often inspired by them.

Many times his words would inspire.

I wanted to follow them.

The characters in the book wandered around alive. I go away thinking that he is an unknown person. Millions of people live in this world. Everyone is always doing something or other. Among them are heroes but few in number.

I thought why is that?

After thinking about rabbits and turtles. Everyone knows the answer.

There is a terrible competition going on all the time. No one is willing to leave a single hair.

Wherever you are today, the success and prosperity of a strictly persevering person is inevitable. One might not like me today. Tomorrow will be ten. Ten thousand after ten years.

Keep trying. Success is just a matter of time. Pay attention to your actions without noticing that you are not paying attention today.

Human acquaintance is in action, not in chatterbox. Going to college, it is seen that many times attempts are made to mislead the students. I have seen many people floating in the current. They are not found today. This is the future, isn't it?

Time speaks.

We have to pay the price for wasting a single moment of life for frustrated and greedy people.

Not everyone can be short-sighted Netaji Subhas Chandra Bose or Vivekananda right, but surely can take himself a long way.

So it is true that despair is expressed in that world but what is its reality?

During my first year of college, everyone would go from house to house in the evenings. After dinner at night, we chat again. He said that studying would be like that. Study started two months before the examination. That was the trend of the hostel. The chat started in my room too. But I do not like it from my heart. I was a studious student. I keep

thinking how to get rid of them! I said a few times to them for study. But it does not work every time.
I thought a lot for some days. Time flees and I become more and more curious about my study as my standard is not improved as per my expectation. I always want to keep myself update with the standard with the Class I am in.
Suddenly I have a trick to get rid of this nonsense.

One day I slap someone on the face during a heated conversation with the mate. In response, I also received several slaps. That's the decent thing to do with them, commensurate with their standard, and it should end there. Thoughts but now the body is thorny.
The exact desired result received.
Since then they have not come to bother. I have no regrets for that trick even today. The persons who misuse their time will never shine in future. It is a universal learning. This is true even in this case. The person who misuses now placed in a lower grade of work, they even today did not able to earn handsome for their family because I am not the birds with the same feather. I am happy for that what I am.
Reason: I learned from my father - "When there is a will there is a way!
These obstacles in life come not to take life backwards, but to enjoy life.
Honest courage is needed in all cases.
No one can stop your success except you.

CHAPTER TWENTY

Firstboy

Michel was then in sixth grade. The results of the mid-term examinations are being published one by one. This year a student has been admitted in the class of Michel. Name Jacob. If you say very good in the study is less said! His father's transfer job. High-ranking government officials. So in this school.

Everyone is humming the Jacob. Even school teachers. Says this time there will be great results in the sixth grade.

What happens in most village high schools. The parents of the students are farmers. Some of the parents are in small government jobs.

Michel's parents and so on. Very poor. Everyone thinks he can do more this year?

The mind has always had a special significance.

He felt a little uncomfortable after that incident. Sometimes it seems that even if he is, this time I am-

However the turn of the results. In science Michel scored seventy-seven, Jocob scored seventy-eight. In Vernacular, Michel eighty and Jacob seventy nine. That's it. No one knows who will be the first.

The results of the sum will come out on that day. Tension. Michel thought he had passed the test well. The teacher is reading out the number obtained by everyone. In a soft, gentle voice, he spoke seventy-seven. Then the turn of the Jacob. The teacher says ninety-nine. About ten times shouting with joy and enthusiasm. Everyone in the class is blessing Jacob. Says this time the Jacob will be the first boy. I am very happy to see the scene. He may think that no one will be able to compete with him this time.

Naturally, because, no one can remember that he got so many marks in his hand. From that day onwards, he often used to bless him while doing arithmetic. The students of the class used to accompany him.

Michel stood second in that time class VI.

He did not learn to lose. He knew he could. Prestige issue but no one can be told. Must havr to prove.

I remember my father's face. Parents can encourage but can't help with studies. His father is a farmer, he is only engaged in farming and raising cows and buffaloes. This is how his day goes.

Meanwhile, Jacob's father took full care of his only son's education.

What an unequal competition! Isn't it?.

"But he is not a loser." - Michel knew.

When he says ninety-nine, he always shouts loudly in his chest. Then he takes a bet to break the bow and if so, why not me?

First of all, analyze in your mind why this spread is different. Easily discovered.

Understand, text books must be well understood. Not completely relying on the notes of the period of blindness given by teachers. The scope of knowledge needs to be widened. Need to work harder as he can. Study strategy needs to change. If necessary, you should read books by different authors on the same subject. You don't have to stop for a moment.

The work that you think.
Today everyone is sitting in the seventh grade room. The masters of that math are making roll calls one by one.
One, Michel Dutt, two, Jacob Roy, three Timothy d'Suza etc.
Absolute satisfaction in the heart of the mind, because he knew "World remembers the winners!"

CHAPTER TWENTY-ONE

The rising sun

Adam's friendship with Kurosawa is about twenty-five years old. He is from Japan. He came to study in this country in the nineties. Now a permanent resident of India. Adam is a successful businessman. Soft-spoken and shy. Respect the wise. Determined man.

But this Adam came from village to town about forty years ago to earn a living. High school side but can speak English well and fluently.

One day he stumbled upon thousands of places and met Kurosawa.

The two of them knew each other very well. Relationships get better day by day.

Influenced by the ideology of Rabindranath Tagore, he came to this country. And education in his ideology.

"Why has his country improved so much?"Adam asked in his mind and he wanted to know about Kurosawa's future plans.

Unequal friendship seems to take a turn for the worse. Towards sustainability.

As humble as he is, his strict discipline, a simple life wrapped in discipline. There is no pride in education and money. Help each other as much as possible. His aquatic example is Adam himself. So she is fascinated.

In that way he understood why their country is so developed, why the average life expectancy of the people of their country is so high and why there is no theft in their country. The more you grieve.

Meanwhile, I am fascinated by Adam's honesty and other good qualities.

This is going on. One day, Kurosawa suddenly said to Adam, "Increase your educational qualifications and get a passport."

He had his eye on the honest and hardworking man from the village. He knew very well that there was no shortage of talent. If the people of this country are given a chance, they will be able to touch the sky. They know how to dream. He puts his life at stake in its implementation. Many times the problem comes. This is normal.

Kurosawa has changed a bit in recent days. It can be understood by Adam. It's as if he wants to say something but can't.

One day Adam wants to know - "What's the matter?"

Suddenly he says, "Japan is thinking of hiring him to a higher position in his company."

The only child of the Kurosawa family because the country has a very low birth rate. People are always engaged in new innovations. Responsibility towards the world is not like our country. They do not bother with words. One of the quietest countries in the world. One hundred percent people are educated. Education is valued there. They all know how to value humanity.

Her father has just passed away. So he has to fulfill the full responsibility of that company.

"I agree! What should I do?" - Said Adam.

"Said nothing."

"Then why?"

Kurosawa said, "There is a strange power among all people in this country. Look! Many people from this country have gone abroad and established their own lives. Everyone knows the names."

Adam has been in Japan for ten years. Corporate meeting tomorrow. Kurosawa will retire.

Adam already knows that he will be the next Chief Executive Officer of the Company.

Adam thinks - "How many people in my country are smarter than me! I think fate depends a lot on karma."

What you think you become! Care should be taken to compete with you not with others. Day by day stiff competition should be maintained within. Step by step, one should improve like a rock. Iron determination should be there with honest approach. Every step should be careful and well maintained and comparable with the time. Boost in morale is the topmost important matter in every aspect.

CHAPTER TWENTY-TWO

Rai Ka hill

People are lined up on both sides of the road. Tears in the eyes of all women. Many are saying in a hushed voice- "Is this the age of his departure. The only son of parents. How calm, polite, elegant, how bright in studies!"

Many are not saying anything but many things are being expressed in body language. Tears flowed from the eyes of some people.

Everyone is praising Smith because he was everyone's favorite. Looks like a prince but has a tender heart.

He was four or five years younger than me. He always talked to me when he met his mother. There was always talking about studying. In that sense, Smith was much loved. They used to call me dear brother. Very polite. I understood that he would be a very much established.

A few days later we moved to another city. I haven't been able to find out for quite some time. I was busy with my work.

You know the girls! When their conversation and friendship started, they found out about each other's pot. Many times the quarrel starts. Does not express in the face, but everything goes in the mind!

Robin is the son of a neighbour. Smith's peers are in the same class. In no case is he equal to Adam. Her parents' nature is to paint everything in color. They are not willing to lose anything. Day goes on like this, night goes on like this.

Sometimes he may say - "Robin has done very well this time. He has got record marks."

Not true at all.

Hearing that, the torture on Smith started.

Her mother used to say- "I don't like to walk around all day long. If you want to eat in this house, you have to read all the time."

Sometimes Robin's father says, "My son was the first to run 100 meters by participating in school sports!"

Maybe not at all.

Hearing that, the torture on Dinesh started again. This time mother and father are both together. In an unspeakable way.

Robin and his parents enjoy watching it.

Smith tried to explain a lot.

Trying to explain a lot to them.

Smith understands how bad the habit of doing 'Rai Ka hill' by dragging a small thing is.

Everyone should understand what is right and what is wrong. Everything can be understood with just a little cool head.

Smith loves his parents so much that he bows down with flowers in their photos and sits for ten minutes. He says to himself - "Forgive me! I will never be able to fulfill your hope. So set me free forever."

He says he makes an extreme decision.

He was the only child of the father. If he had survived, he would have been about thirty-five years old. The foolishness of the parents and the deceit of the neighbors did not spare a single child.

When her mother saw me, she still cried in front of them. Her father is almost mad. A deception that is the death of a child.

So parents have to be careful when dealing with their children, otherwise -

Alas! When people think about where they are today, they feel insulted.

(Rai ka hill - The word is Hindi, meaning to consider irrelevant or unimportant things as extra important.)

CHAPTER TWENTY-THREE

On the way to eternity

I am sitting on the second floor. There is a vision towards the path of that pond. Thinking about it, Touche enters the world of imagination. After two or three hours, my father would come with a stick in his hand.

Growing up, one day he was admitted to the city for higher studies.

During the holidays he came back and stared at the path of the pond for a while. Soap and oil were used for bathing, he become very happy in it. While taking a bath, he heard a woman from the next house abusing him. The matter was not understood by him. He becomes curious and he wanted to know that in details. He is now quite mature in it. It is nothing wrong to know the exact reason behind it.

I wanted to know my mother!

He said - "What's the matter mother? Why is Sion's mother talking like that?"

Mother said - "Alas! You didn't have to be told. There is a lot of unrest in the neighborhood along the way to the pond. Eventually there were fights and fights. The signers claimed the road as their own.

Touche was very upset to hear that. Didn't say anything. He just said to his mother- "Okay! Let's eat."

He has never been there since. Year after year has passed.

Sion's mother has passed away. Now no one goes there just like that. Dirty, bushy jungle.
In the past, people used to bathe in that water, wash dishes and that water was used for household purposes.
After that incident, people no longer use that water.
Touche looks that way and why is he so arrogant?!
What's so significant about a goat's head ?!
Why so much unrest?!
In the course of time, everything ends one day. All that remains is human use and work done for human beings.
All the time if someone does what I do and eats - responsibility and eventually dies then what is the value of his life?
Even an animal does these things.
People's personalities and understanding have set people apart.
Touche looks at the sky and thought hell and heaven. It become afternoon as the time fly.
Mother called from below - "Touche, its tea time."

CHAPTER TWENTY-FOUR

Born to exist

"I kept saying this. I am the daughter of one father. I will never see your face again for life. Let's see if my family can survive without your help. Annie's eyes watered profusely as he spoke. The throat is trembling. The right side of the body seems to be numb.

Annie and Sassy's conflict would almost be the same again. The people of the area thought it was their common heart signature. After Sassy's mother passed away in her childhood, that bond seemed to become stronger.

Sassy's family is relatively rich. But neither Sassy's father nor any of her family ever let Annie know. Annie and everyone in the house thought she was a relative. The two had free association. The two of them used to eat and drink together a lot of the time. That's how the two of them grew up. Entering youth from childhood. Companion of all joys and sorrows. Twenty-two years seem to have passed in an instant. How much happiness is the companion of sorrow? The two have learned to share everything together. Both were essential parts of each other.

The first verse was cut when Annie was offered marriage by a family. The boy is highly educated, elegant and earning. The boy liked Sassy again.

After a little trouble, Annie's happy marriage was

consummated with him.

Since her marriage, Sassy feels alone. The two most beautiful flowers in the world seem to be separated. In the middle of the night, Sassy dreams that Annie, the subconscious mind, can't accept their separation. Suddenly she woke up with difficulty. The love between them was unadulterated and pure. How did Annie forget her after getting a good family in her mind and way? Tears well up in her eyes as she thinks about these things. Everything gradually became normal for Sassy. Because human are a slave to habit.

In this way one day offer for Sassy's marriage come. In your own neighbourhood.

Meanwhile, Annie's father died suddenly.

That's how the two girlfriends met again.

Since there was no problem between them, the bond was strengthened again.

The real problem started with Sassy's mother-in-law. She did not like that meeting at all. She thought what was before marriage, was. What again?

She said a few times. Annie doesn't want to accept anything.

That's why today she says to Sassy- "Grandma. Tell Annie a little, I can't find my left ear-ring ! I left it in that room. I can't find it. Annie was alone in that room when you went to the bathroom. . '"Saying this, she burst into tears. This skillful performance of the mother-in-law but Sassy did not notice and imagine at all.

Necessarily the ultimate decision.

For one, that sweet relationship is over.

"How are you?"

Where time and circumstances have changed them. The people of the magical country are scattered through no

change.
They had a rhythmic life. Like the rhythm of poetry. It's like cutting a rhythm.
Both of them are suffering in their minds for this event but none can realize the actual reason behind and become very sorry thinking about them.
They both deal with their confidence as they choose to embark on their play activities. To be worldly. The emergence of a new generation comes to mind. They both have beautiful family and husband. They become so much absorbed in it that they forget the past. Their childish friendships become not necessary to continue. I have a good number of well-wishers who continuously helped me during my hardship and now there is no need to get any types of support from anybody. As we live in the society where person think for their immediate relatives. Care to them.

It is very important to remember that-" Out of sight is out of mind." This proved true in this case also. The two full grown ladies, all of sudden come into reality and involved in the present relations.
In their minds they both want to forget the past. The words of that pure girl.
Now only omnipotent selfishness continues.

CHAPTER TWENTY-FIVE

Looking for a little warmth

Good name Jacobine. At first him father started calling him 'Jacob'. From then on, he became known as Jacob. He stayed in our neighborhood. Two small houses. Straw shed in the house. There are no windows in any house. Doors are simply made of tin. Dogs and cats are kept away from it, not thieves. There are seven animals in that house, big and small. He has parents, a brother, a wife and a son and a daughter. The girl is eleven years old and the boy is three. The girl is very naughty, the boy is just as calm.

I have no idea how they live in this place. What comes to you?

Jacob lives on daily wages. His own health is his only capital. Jacob is a very calm person. So almost everyone in the neighbourhood calls him for their housework and pays him a fair wage.

As he lives on food and mouth, it is as if he has become old at a young age. Unshaven beard all the time on the face. Uncut hair on the head. Three days ago he was told to work at home. It is found that there is no instance to come in late, but No day is too late to come to work but today came about half an hour later. As if calm. Occasionally wiping

away tears a little more quietly. What a little impression!
"The south wall of the house has to be finished today," says Michel.
Jacob is almost nine years younger than Michel. It looks like the opposite. As the saying goes, "Much depends on money. Respect, influence, prestige, longevity. The power of money is infinite."
I thought just the opposite.
Wake up but stay quite happy the other day. Occasionally, he would say something funny and save the meeting.
Throughout the day he was a little less focused on his work. The matter seemed to stall. So before paying the wages in the afternoon I wanted to know what is the matter?
Grandpa said nothing. Tears welled up in his eyes as he insisted.
I said, "What happened?"
He said without expression: "My little boy is gone! He has a high fever for seven days now. He has no money to eat at home. Hence, I can't even visit a doctor. Then there are no warm clothes to read in winter. I'm completely broken down. I don't know what else to do. "
"What do you say? Hey, tell me?" - Michel got scared.
"Grandpa! Have you done much? And no!" - The answer came.
I felt guilty in my mind. I wondered why we don't give ourselves and our boys and girls some warm clothes to people like them. Many are destroyed. They are useful to them. Everyone has the right to life in this world. People like Jacob will end up still not wanting anything to get their hands on anyone. Do not go astray. Will end up on its own if necessary.
They will never surrender to their self-esteem.
I think to myself - "We need them at the wrong time. I think

of people like them. Stand by them. It will not be bad at all." Of course, some people will be able to put a smile on the faces of some children and the elderly in this severe winter. Our tender heart must be warm if we come a little further. What do you say?

We probably think for ourselves too much and at the end of the day we become too much selfish and do not think for other. There are the people who can not earn much for their family because of lack of scope. They, too, have little children. They have family, father, wife, and above all wish to flurish in the future for betterment of future. In this juncture, we can lend our hand for little benefit of the others. The world, then, will be more beautiful for human. These people and their family will also be happier for these reason. There will be no harm in it.

CHAPTER TWENTY-SIX

The breadwinner; My life

"It's sunny today. I haven't sunk the paddy yet. What can I do with you?" He knows very well that if it is not dried properly now, there will be no good seedlings from that paddy in drought. And if you have to buy seedlings, you will not be able to plant rice in drought.

How a farmer like him, who has no other income, spends his family, I think is an important part of university research.

Unable to stay, I went to Samuel and found out many things. They said we had a lot of land. Earlier the yield was low but I did not use inorganic chemical fertilizers. The total would be compensated. We were young; we used to do almost all the land work by ourselves. There was no plow in the house. So on the whole, the family has passed well then.

Don't talk about it now brother! You can see.

Saying this, he started cleaning the paddy again with the air of by some handmade bamboo craft.

The condition of villages, blacksmiths, potters, weavers and other handicrafts has changed since the introduction of machine-operated machines.

Those who can keep pace with the times can survive

through the ages. Many popular and sustainable things in the laws of nature still survive. It's too late!
People are born to do their duty. Many times they deliberately reveal different parts of their life, many times he deliberately hides his needs. Comes and goes. Civilization survives when you are exposed to glory.
Now almost everyone seems to express everything in an artificial way. Child-friendly agility can be seen?
Social culture, entertainment, everything seems to have become artificial. Where have people lost themselves? Forgetting the service of humanity.
Humanity dies when I see the breadwinner weeping for money, even when he can't cultivate his life twice.
In fact, the cow in the story never climbs a tree.
What is happening to a group of people without everyone's knowledge -
Everyone seems to need a little thought again.
It is in the interest of all of us that these Samuel survive in peace. Only then will humanity sound the trumpet of victory. That must be today or tomorrow.

CHAPTER TWENTY-SEVEN

From the pages of history

The Goddess of wealth to live in trade.
half of that in agriculture .
half of that in public service.
nothing in begging.
(A sanskrit verse)

Preparations have begun for the ascension of Emperor Chandragupta Maurya to the throne. It's time to dump her and move on. Everyone is giving their own opinion on how to make this ceremony better or more memorable.

Oddly enough Chanakya or Kautilya is missing.

Chandragupta Maurya asked-- "Where is Kautilya?"

No one could give a reasonable answer. He sensed some conspiracy on it. Hence, Chandragupta Maurya immediately announced the cancellation of the meeting and decided to hold it the next afternoon. He also announced that Kautilya must be present at that gathering. This is the Kautilya who is equally famous as Chanakya in Indian history. He authored a book, Arthashastra, also known as "Kautilya's Arthashastra".

Dhanananda was the last king and oppressor of the Nanda dynasty. That dynasty was dynasty was set up by famous ruler called Mahapadnanda. One day Dhanananda insulted Kautilya without any fair reason. He was severely humiliated in that incident. He was a learned person with high intellect.

On that day he took in the mind that he would give befitting reply to Dhanananda for such humiliation.

Not much is known after that. Only a little is known that he made the boy Chandragupta suitable for the king by teaching him various subjects including how to use different weapons available at that time. During this time of these severe training, two individual one of them was Chandragupta Murya were equally prominent for the post of the king. Chanakya, the great, become very thoughtful about that matter.

He had an experiment to solve a slight dilemma.

Chandragupta was the equal of Maurya in courage and strength. The main point of the test was to find out who was the better of the two.

So he called the two of them separately and gave them two amulets and instructed them to recite it. They both wore it in the neck. Then a few days later he called the two of them separately and said to the two of them- "He will think that he is the best one who can give him back two amulets without informing the other!"

Chandragupta returned the amulet to Chanakya by killing another while he was asleep.

This is that great Chanakya who was not invited to the annexation ceremony.

Maurya knew that the world was full of bastards and greedy people. They go around all the time for the purpose of their existence and money. It's amazing how many years ago it was equally true.

The history of these greedy people is not remembered.

They are lost with the passage of time. We do not know their names even after trying. Isn't it?

We too can easily recognize almost all people in this way.

The next day the meeting took place as scheduled. That Chandragupta appointed Kautilya as his chief of staff and prime minister.

The Kautilya's physique was not good. The ugly man is a rare star in the history of the world. His erudition is admired all over the world. He is equally famous as Vishnugupta.

Day by day the Mauryan empire continued to prosper and become one of the famous in the world. His knowledge is also appreciated in the world. Kautilya's policy was followed by Emperor Chandragupta Maurya and other Maurya emperors like Bindusara and Ashoka the great. Historians have rightly identified it as one of the glorious chapters of India at that time. Kautilya's association with the Nanda dynasty's incompetence is incomparable. One of the strangest competitions in history. One rise and one fall. Each of his verses is famous because it contains everything including respect, knowledge and pure truth and caution towards people from all walks of life.

This chapter of Indian history is not only educative for the world but also highly appreciated by the people all across of the life and world. It is well appreciated also.

CHAPTER TWENTY-EIGHT

Conflict: Russia and Ukraine

We all know that Russia is a super-power. It is the largest country in the world even after disintegration of Union of Soviet Socialist Republics (USSR) that was a socialist state that spanned Eurasia during its existence from 1922 to 1991. The country was a one-party state (prior to 1990) governed by the Communist Party of the Soviet Union, with Moscow as its capital within its largest and most populous republic, the Russian SFSR. Other major centers were Leningrad (Russian SFSR), Kyiv or Kiev (Ukrainian SSR), Minsk (Byelorussian Soviet Socialist Republics), Tashkent (Uzbekistan Soviet Socialist Republic), Alma-Ata (Kazakhastan Soviet Socialist Republics) and Novosibirsk (Russian SFSR). It was the largest country in the world, covering over 22,402,200 square kilometers (8,649,500 sq mile), and spanning eleven time zones. It is also highest by any country.

After the disintegration at 1991, the largest part was Russia. They also considered as global super power because they have different kinds of missile(both Cruise and ballistic) that are often considered as best of its kind. They have fighter get, multi-role aircraft and S-400 and other protective missile defense systems that are also considered as world's best. They earn a huge amount of foreign reserve from arms and ammunition export. They are major exporter of technology related to such field. They developed Brahmas cruise missile system jointly with India. This is also considered standard and world's best of its kind. They have aircraft carrier and many more. It is worth to say that the Kyiv is situated by the side of the Dnieper River.

So, question comes how and why a small country like Ukraine has involved in conflict with Russia.

Different person and specialists gave their different views. There should be a balance of power. The North Atlantic Treaty Organization (NATO) and its allies constantly bother their interest in respect of their safety and security. Here, the present Ukranian President Volodymyr Zelenskyy constantly tries to become a part of NATO to secure the safety of their country but Vladimir Putin the present president of Russia constantly oppose that move because these will become the different power centre for the Western Country like USA, UK and so on.

As Ukraine was the part of earlier USSR and many citizen of this country even today is Russian language speaking, so they secretly helped Russia.

In February and March 2014, Russia invaded and subsequently annexed the Crimean Peninsula from Ukraine. This event took place in the aftermath of the Revolution of Dignity and is part of the wider Russo-Ukrainian conflict. After that a bridge was constructed (Crimean Bridge). Construction works started in February 2016 and completed in April 2018 (Road Bridge) December 2019 (Rail Bridge) with a whooping cost of 227.92 billion rubles. Since the inception, the Ukraine opposes it. To maintain the supremacy of the region in present and future, Russia is believed to take this action.

Russia wants country like Belarus who always accept its supremacy openly and act like a friendly country from where there is no immediate threat for them.

The Ukrainian president constantly oppose the Russia for different angles and accumulate arms and ammunition and other military equipment form different NATO allies which sometimes eye sore for the Russia. Sometime the President of USA and the Prime Minister of UK and some world leader gave some speeches in favour of Ukraine and against Russia which sometimes the Ukrainian Prez greatly motivated and took strong stand against Russia.

As, Putin was highly talented and have great experiences in politics, took advantage of this situation and took steps to disarm the Ukraine through military exercise. He included his plan to support the separatists at Donbas region. Donbas (Don-BAS) This word refers to the region of southeastern Ukraine that includes Donetsk and Luhansk. The term "Donbas" is an acronym, which means "Donets coal basin, Donetsk, formerly known as Aleksandrovka, Yuzivka, Stalin and Stalino, is an industrial city in eastern Ukraine located on the Kalmius River.

On 22 February 2022, the Ministry of Foreign Affairs published a statement welcoming the recognition of independence of the Donetsk and Luhansk People's Republics by Russian President Vladimir Putin.

Luhansk and formerly known as Voroshilovgrad (Ukrainian and Russian:1935–1958 and 1970–1990), is a city in eastern Ukraine, near the border with Russia in the disputed Donbas region. Luhansk is currently the capital and administrative center of the Luhansk People's Republic (LPR), a breakaway state, established in 2014 by pro-

Russian separatists.

Russia has launched a large-scale invasion of Ukraine on 24 February 2022 and meanwhile NATO ,USA and others have declined to support Ukraine militarily. The strikes of Russia included missile attacks and Aerial an cyber attacks. Three types of attacks like Military, Aerial and Naval forces of Russia were used in this invasion. The Russian forces consciously targeted only to the forces of Ukraine and they as much as they can exclude the public. The main aim of Russia in the invasion is to fall the Kyiv and present political system of Ukraine and create a favourable environment for Russia. Several collateral damages are also reported.

There were several cyber attacks on Russian government website perhaps done by Ukraine or some friendly organizations. The situation of these events increases the gravity of the conflict which becomes more dangerous for the world at large. Several countries in the world although not involved in the conflict directly, but assisted Ukraine by providing security assistance, fund, intelligence, several kinds of arm and ammunitions, foods and other logistics. This somehow boosts the mental strength of Ukraine. Both the military and militia become active to save the Ukraine at any cost from the Russia. The whole world particularly the west is now sympathize to Ukraine. The normal citizen is found to be digging trenches in the road and they said to prevent the normal passage of the battle tanks. From both sides, there were claims and counter claims about the damage done by the rival parties. It is particularly said to be a propaganda for the both the sides. There is no time to find the exact truth right at the present, which serves the purpose of the originator of these. The Turkey has involved as in 2019, Baykar Makina, a privately owned Turkish drone maker, won a contract to sell six Bayraktar TB2 UAVs to Ukraine. The $69 million contract also involved the sale of ammunition for the armed version of the aircraft. These drones have extensively used to counter the Russian attack on Ukraine. Its utility in the field of war is very pertinent. This may play a decisive role in determining the fate of a war.

Meanwhile, USA, Canada, Japan, European Union (27 members of the EU at present) and other countries of the world imposed economic and several other types of sanctions to Russia. It is pertinent to say here that the Black Sea region is particularly very rich in natural gas and several other mineral. Several countries of Europe heavily depend on this natural resources. So before, doing anything detrimental to Russia, care should be taken in this aspect also. If the Russia, who poses this huge natural resources may take stern action by stopping the delivery of these. So, logically, Russia is now in a little advantageous position. There was a voting in United Nations Security Council. They took up the draft resolution condemning the Russian invasion in the early hours of Saturday, 26th February 2022. The result of the vote was 11-1-3. The Security Council Fails to Adopt Draft Resolution on Ending Ukraine Crisis, as Russian Federation Wields Veto. As we know that the United Nations Security Council "veto power" is the power of the five permanent members of the UN Security Council (China, France, Russia, the United Kingdom, and the United States) to veto any "substantive" resolution. India, China and UAE are the countries who abstain from the voting. As a result of the crisis that Russian currency Ruble drops nearly 40% in comparison to USD. [1 Russian Ruble= 0.012 USD as on 28th February 2022]. Several economic restrictions that imposed by different countries also become activated and acted against this Russia. It is certainly an unique event which is totally unprecedented. The economic system of Russia has a badly hit. Meanwhile, in Ukraine as a result of strike, the different types of human installations, public building, petrol pumps and several other important places either fully or partly destroyed. In Ukraine, the Chernobyl Nuclear Power Plant Zone of Alienation is an officially designated exclusion zone around the site of the Chernobyl nuclear reactor disaster. It is also commonly known as the Chernobyl Exclusion Zone[CEZ], the 30-Kilometre Zone, or simply 'The Zone". This place also become under the control of Russia due to the in invasion. Subsequently, the Russian troops announced that they had taken control of Europe's biggest nuclear power plant Zaporizhzhia, situated in the Ukraine. The International Atomic Energy Agency (IAEA) should be cautious in this respect.

There was a peace talk in the Belarus on 28 February 2022 between Ukraine and Russia to negotiate the crisis. The result of the peace talks does not confirmed initially. Russia on the other hand threatened to use nuclear or atom bomb during this conflict. This should be taken very seriously as this not only be a mere threatening but also be a strategy of the Russian warfare. It was found that the peace talk, if we termed it as first round, had no immediate result. Meanwhile, the Russia has intensified the attack in Ukraine mainly to the major cities like in Kyiv and Kharkiv. The cause of the attack on Ukraine by the Russia which subsequently converted into the war was very clear. So, eventually, the worst sufferers were the citizen of that country. Some students or other common personnel who had come to Ukraine from different reasons like wage laborers, engineers, doctors, or some other professions become badly hit. Some of them even lost their life. It is particularly bad instance for the humanity at large.

It is very much pertinent to state that every countries of the world have the right to think for their citizen first. So, none of the country have engaged in the conflict directly. It is good for the world also. As a result of that this particular conflict did not spread to the other countries of the world till now. In the long run, how much, it will be possible to restrain that cannot be ascertained right now but this event is truly unique for the world. Some of the counties like USA and Germany have helped the Ukraine through direct funding or artillery. If we discuss it in details behind this, several reasons will come into surface, it may be humanitarian and also may be passively resist Russia, the country want to establish it's supremacy in the world. A very thin line is there to understand the actual reason behind. So, if the conflicts continue for the larger time, two types of things will come into surface. i) The Russia will be weaker in terms of economic power which will directly affect its military power. These consequences will help other developed to establish their supremacy in long run in the future. As the Russia will be out of this race as their internal citizen's need will be their first priority. It will be the automatic normal choice. ii) If they help the Ukraine by passive means, they will resist the Russia for the longer time (days). The result of the conflict may change the face of the people of this country. So, in long run, only the both country will badly suffer. They need more time to normalize the situation. In this conflict, some of the country may be benefitted that should not be encouraged as this costs several human's life and property. It is sad but it is the bitter truth that none can deny. A large number of the Ukrainian people have fled from this country. They mainly moved to Poland, Hungary, Romania, Bulgaria, Slovakia, and Russia. So, the adjoining countries now faced crisis of refugee and if it continues for a longer period, these problem will manifest acute crisis over these population. The fate of these refugees will be determined by the existing laws of these countries. Sometimes, apparently very detrimental effect will be waited for the future. These points should be seriously taken into account for peaceful co-existence of the society.

Meanwhile, the second round of talks between Russia and Ukraine is planned for March 2, 2022. This peace talk was also failed to a great extent. It is not only bad for the common people of Ukraine but also for the people of the world. The massive damage that the people witnessed in different cities of Ukraine cannot be justified along with the severe loss of human life. In history, we have found so much genocide in different countries but in these instant cases, this is particularly unique in nature because these are two European countries mainly inhabited by highly cultured and educated people.

It is expected to the Russia that they took the control of Khariv and Kharsan of Ukraine. Now they have intensified the attack in Kyiv. In this juncture, Russia has been accused of planning to use thermo baric weapons - also known as vacuum bombs - in its invasion of Ukraine. These are controversial because they are much more devastating than conventional explosives of similar size, and have a terrible impact on anyone caught in their blast radius.

How a vacuum bomb works, as per expert opinion, many defense expert says-

The vacuum bomb often called an aerosol bomb or fuel air explosive consists of a fuel container with two separate explosive charges. The two containers have different distinctive roles during their operations. they can be launched as a rocket or dropped as a bomb from aircraft. As these hit there target, the first explosive charge opens the container and widely scatters fuel mixture as a cloud. This is truely devastating. This cloud can penetrate any building openings or defences that are not totally sealed. A second charge then detonates the cloud, resulting in a huge fireball, a massive blast wave and a vacuum which sucks up all surrounding oxygen. The weapon can destroy reinforced buildings, equipment and kill or injure people.

There are a number of countries who either directly or indirectly involved in the conflict. We cannot deny the effect of the it. The share market of almost all countries crushed in the fear of it. The import and import of the countries badly hit. The crude oil price has reached into the maximum. A material cascading effect has touched everyone. The price of the commodities has increased day after day. As India is the major exporter of arms and ammunition from Russia, the dependency still loom large.

During the time of the conflict, both the Russia and the Ukraine should have their strategies for the future. The Russia who is the highest nuclear armour holder has specific strategy and after the invasion, they specifically targeted the cities ahead. They gradually intensified the attack along with the target with the massage to the world. The other countries that although not participated in the conflict have some specific interest. They for that reasons have articulated in these specific ways.

In is quite obvious in the present context, the Ukraine, the country which is neither comparable with the Russia in military power nor any artillery power, have resisted them in a spectacular way and gave the world an instance to love the motherland. It is needless to say that the result of this conflict is predetermined. There should be more talk with the rival countries and more care should have been taken to avoid the needles conflict. There is a huge destruction of infrastructure both public and private in the Ukrainian side. There was much civilian causality which should not have been. The economy of the country is not good at all. So based on the thought, the Ukraine should evade this. Their priority should be more pragmatic not emotional as it costs heavily and this country will lag behind at least fifty year in the future. The Asian countries like India and China along with the American countries will be far ahead in days to come.

I personally don't understand how and why the Ukraine want to stand for confront the Russia. It would be definitely considered as one of the poorest failed politics by a head of the state not only for a modern European history but also for rest of the world. For the gross failure by a head of the state, entire Ukrainian people suffer that is truly unparallel. As a result of the conflict, presently Russia who now stands second in the power position may fail to continue its position in near future and the other countries mainly like the China and India may continue to speed up their progress. It would ultimately become the new world order that the world would see. The China is already few steps ahead of India.

With a lots of hope in future, it is expected that this conflict will not ends up to a great (Notorious ?) war that will emancipate into cause of millions of death as it was caused into WW-II.

CHAPTER TWENTY-NINE

The goal of life

Kneith is sitting in the yard today. Mirror in hand. Looking at the face in the mirror and smiling just like people do when taking selfies. Visualization of one's own form from different gestures and different angles. I like myself in that picture. Laughs again.

Adam noticed this from the door for a while and in his mind Dada doesn't do that. Something must have happened, Grandpa.

Adam and Kneith are two brothers. Adam is about twelve years younger than him. Kneith is 27 years old. He has just finished his studies. The result is quite good. I never think of anything other than studying.

That is, target study.

Adam always tries to follow his elder brother. His elder brother also tries to help him enough.

Generation gap between the two brothers is an era! Or what! Everyone says twelve years is one era. Not so.

What do you say? Age or something else.

Then job or business. Dad owns a big electronics business. The other person is running it, instead he has to pay big money.

So let his father's target Kneith take over the business.

Kneith wants to do government job. Now this is his target.

Adam wants to go to a good school for higher education in a good city.

Their mother wants to bring a wife home with the marriage of her eldest son.

Just think! What is the target of four people in the house? How many types?

But everyone is always planning like him to get his target.

Some people work hard and some people cheat.

The one who lacks diligence in his plan delays or fails to meet his target.

This target may be forced to change from time to time by every human being knowingly or unknowingly. This is the infallible law of nature.

The moon, the sun all meet their own targets. The month of the moon, the day of the earth and the year of the sun.

So every human being should always have an honest target.

This nature is such that everyone is bound to obey him.

It is the job of the teacher in the school to educate the students and gradually develop their knowledge. Again, government officials have to complete their own work, this is some of their work.

Every time we find ourselves, knowingly or unknowingly, we are busy fulfilling a target.

Every object of nature is always moving in the same formula. As water moves from top to bottom. When iron is heated, it turns red and hot. The sound is made by beating with a tin stick.

That is, an exact result is predetermined for each action.

We all understand this. Many times it is difficult to accept.

Despite knowing so much, most of the time we don't target anything.

Then don't think about how our target will be met.

What a truth. Not so.

Think and fulfill the target. Target again and keep working for it again. By doing so, you will surely occupy an honorable place. That nature itself is ready to give you.

It's just a matter of time.

The human race is the best of nations. Yet we despise nature above all else.

Whose toll and we pay.

Life without a target is a lot like a kite without a rope. Can't fly!

Similarly, people cannot reach any goal. In human life it is an invisible rope. Not to be seen but of course necessary.

CHAPTER THIRTY

The fruit of hard work

Let's enter a world of imagination today. Just stay there. No night. Sunlight is always circulating. Everything is like the earth but there is no decay of anything. There is no destruction, so there is no creation.

All people are educated in higher education. If necessary, they can travel to another planet through time travel.

All people have understood the nature of God so there is no unrest and violence. Oddly enough people have reached the pinnacle of development.

Discovering new things is an ongoing campaign for the ultimate victory of humanity.

Not great. It's something we haven't even dreamed of.

Well what if it is ever possible?

It is surprising to think. No one is poor but everyone is intelligent. No one can be fooled easily.

Have you ever wondered which class of people will be harmed if it continues like this?

Yes! You have caught those hypocrites. Whose purpose is to satisfy their own interests by taking advantage of other people's ignorance.

So the first and foremost purpose of all should be to give real education to the people. Improving the quality of education in a difficult way.

Education brings consciousness. Renaissance brings consciousness. Renaissance brings liberation. Freedom from superstition, freedom from ignorance, freedom from want, freedom from unrest, freedom from restlessness or instability. Opens a new direction.

One class of people therefore always wants the betterment of people of all walks of life. Everyone works for humanity. Today's society recognizes them as philosophers, mathematicians, scholars, writers or scientists. Their only goal is to be good to people of all walks of life. All of them are doing their best. They don't want any fame or anything else.

They are intoxicated with the joy of creation. The world has advanced for them. They are, they were and they will be. For ages.

They are steadfast in their goal. Their strange personality and wisdom has been exposing and overwhelming all through the ages. The existence of God is there.

It is for them that human society has come so far and will improve. Will go to an extreme peak of improvement.

Who said God does not meet. He is one of them.

And those who provide these barriers are none other than -----!

Truth has always prevailed. Here it will be.

Society will follow its own rules. All animals and plants, including humans, are slaves to the law.

So people are slowly moving towards that imaginary world. Towards an infinite immortality.

God is with us all the time. With truth and with beauty.

So that victory drum is still flying.

Printed by Libri Plureos GmbH in Hamburg, Germany